PICTURING SCOTLAND

THE OUTER HEBRIDES

NESS PUBLISHING

2   The island of Benbecula is situated between North Uist and South Uist. It is a place of many lochs and lochans which can dramatically reflect the light at either end of the day.

THE OUTER HEBRIDES

Welcome to the Outer Hebrides!

Among the many worlds of Scotland, the Outer Hebrides (or Western Isles) must be one of the most other-worldly realms of this diverse nation. Lying off the north-west coast of Scotland, this archipelago of over 200 islands stretches around 130 miles from north to south.

The 15 inhabited islands support a resident population of about 26,500, making this region one of the least densely populated parts of Scotland. Despite great differences between the various islands, what they have in common is water – lots of it! This watery world contains over 6,000 lochs. Small wonder then that the Outer Hebrides are also abundant in a great variety of wildlife: seabirds, freshwater birds, seals, otters and whales can all be seen on and around the islands. Low-lying western coastal areas are the location of the machair, the grassy dune-land formed by wind-blown shell sand from around 3000BC onwards, which comes alive in spring with a carpet of flowers.

This is indeed another world, separated by more than sea from mainland Scotland. Here, the voices of the distant past still speak loud and clear through the numerous remnants of ancient societies. Traces of the Neolithic, Bronze and Iron Ages rub shoulders in vying for our attention.

The machair: a close look at some of the flowers that make up this colourful carpet   5
in spring and early summer. Inset: a clover flower in detail.

Stone circles, standing stones, brochs and burial cairns can be found in abundance throughout the islands. The main focus of Neolithic activity is the astonishing network of stone circles in and around Calanais. The principal site presents an awesome array of intricately arranged stones that grips the attention of visitors from all over the world.

Early Christian sites also abound, dating from the 6th century onwards. Evidence of the Norse empire is plentiful in place names and archaeological remains. The Gaels, present long before the Norse invaders, managed to survive the tenure of these overlords (which ended in 1266) and today their culture remains a major influence. The Gaelic language is still widely spoken and the islands' indigenous music has developed an international following.

The Outer Hebrides are now officially known by their Gaelic name, Na h-Eileanan Siar. Indeed, the Gaelic names for all the islands take precedence on official signage, so it is useful to know what they are when travelling. Therefore, they are included in brackets in the following paragraph which sets out the plan of this book. Although they look very different in Gaelic, their pronunciation is similar to the English.

6   A carving thought to be of St Clement in Rodel church (see pages 44/45).

Our photographic tour begins in Stornoway (Steòrnabhagh), the capital of the islands, located on the east coast of the island of Lewis (Leòdhais). From here it explores the northern reaches of Lewis before heading south-west to the antiquity-laden area around Callanish (Calanais). A trip to the island of Great Bernera follows, then south to Harris (Na Hearadh), the mountainous heart of the northern half of the Outer Hebrides. Although Lewis and Harris are thought of as separate islands, they are in fact one landmass divided by a land border. Beyond Harris a ferry crossing takes us to the southern group of islands. From north to south these are Berneray (Bhearnaraigh), North Uist (Uibhist a Tuath), Benbecula (Beinn na Faoghla), South Uist (Uibhist a Deas), and Eriskay (Eiriosgaigh). These islands are all linked by a series of causeways, but from Eriskay the final stage of our tour entails another ferry to reach Barra (Eilean Bharraigh) and Vatersay (Bhatarsaigh).

This remote western edge of Scotland exudes a world-between-worlds atmosphere, a place where a maritime environment embraces a land of ancient mystery, a land in which resident and visitor alike will succumb to its matchless, moody magnificence.

Stornoway War Memorial floodlit.   7

8 Stornoway viewed from Gallows Hill. Lews Castle, built in 1848 for Sir Charles Matheson and later the home of Lord Leverhulme, can be seen on the left. Stornoway grew up around the best natural

harbour in the Outer Hebrides. Regular ferries serve Stornoway from Ullapool on the mainland. The town is a good base from which to explore Lewis. It also hosts an annual Celtic Festival.

10 The waterfront at Stornoway. The building towards the left with clocktower is the Old Town Hall. Towards the right with the pink and black turret is An Lanntair, the arts centre.

Seals are a fairly common sight on the more remote Outer Hebridean coasts, but this one 11 was spotted in Stornoway harbour, keeping an eye on the photographer!

12 Left: Stornoway's harbour hosts many pleasure craft and fishing boats and a Lifeboat is also stationed there. Right: the beautifully crafted Herring Girl statue by the harbour.

The Eye Peninsula stretches east from Stornoway, seen here from across Broad Bay. Tiumpan Head **13** lighthouse is just visible on the left. Hebridean weather often provides dramatic skyscapes like this.

14 In 1919, returning servicemen confronted the then owner of Lewis, Lord Leverhulme, over the issue of land tenure rights. This memorial at Gress (north-west of Stornoway) commemorates these events.

From Gress the road goes to the village of Tolsta, beyond which lies this rugged stretch of coast, **15** so typical of Lewis. But Tolsta also has a fine beach, well-worth a visit.

16 The road continues a mile or so beyond Tolsta, after which a track leads to this waterfall. Wet weather had dramatically increased the flow over the falls when this picture was taken.

Moving now to the northern-most tip of Lewis, this is the attractive haven of the Port of Ness. **17**
This is an area in which Gaelic is the language of choice for many people.

18 Nearby is the Butt of Lewis, the most northerly point of the island, with its famous lighthouse. Established in 1862, it stands 37 metres high and its light can be seen from a distance of 25 nautical miles.

The Butt has appeared in the Guinness Book of Records as the windiest spot in the UK. Even on relatively calm days, like this, the sea crashes with force on the rocks around the lighthouse.

20 Left: the straight and narrow way that leads to St Moluag's Church at Eoropie, close to the Butt of Lewis. Right: A stained glass window in the church. St Moluag was a contemporary of St Columba.

Eoropie beach – simply fabulous! There are several more beach scenes in this book, but that is because **21**
they are such a feature throughout the Outer Hebrides, and they all just beg to be photographed!

22 Similarly, ancient remains are plentiful. Left: Clach an Truiseil, the tallest standing stone in Scotland at almost 6m/20ft high. Right: remains of the Neolithic chambered cairn at Steinacleit.

This 'blackhouse' at Arnol on the north-west coast of Lewis was occupied until 1964, yet its architecture and layout follow a tradition that goes back to the Viking period.

24 This is the main grouping of stones at Calanais (Calanais 1), work on which began around 2900BC. It consists of around 50 stones, comprising a circle with central monolith (middle of picture) and straight

lines of stones that run approximately north, south, east and west from the circle. The remains of a burial chamber can be seen inside the circle, with four small stones remaining upright (see also pages 30/31).

26 Left: inside the Arnol blackhouse, complete with peat fire and spinning wheel. Right: interior of the restored Norse water-powered grain mill at Shawbost, showing the grain hopper and grindstone.

Shawbost lies a few miles west of Arnol. The building on the right houses the mill equipment **27** shown opposite, while the nearer building to the left contains a drying kiln.

28 Continuing south-west brings us to Garenin (Gearrannan) where blackhouse restoration has been taken a stage further, with a small village of such houses. Here, a stack of peat is drying in readiness for winter.

Brochs are among Scotland's most impressive prehistoric buildings. Dun Carloway is a particularly **29** well-preserved example. It provided a defensible dwelling for the principal family of the area.

30 Returning to Calanais, this is Cnoc Fillibhir Bheag (Calanais 3), one of 11 further groups of standing stones located around the vicinity of the main group, making this a veritable metropolis of ritual sites.

A visit to Calanais can be rewarding at any time of year, as the seasons all bring their own light and moods to the stones. The Calanais Visitor Centre offers insights into the story behind the stones.

32 After Calanais, a visit to the isle of Great Bernera is an essential detour. Keeping right on to the end of the road at Bosta presents views like this of the skerries and stacks of this wild landscape.

The weather is prone to sudden change – so be prepared to embrace whatever it throws at you! For **33** example, a family enjoys sunshine on the beach, while beyond the sea is rough as the storm approaches.

34 Leaving Lewis behind, we venture south to mountainous Harris. Here are the highest hills in the Outer Hebrides, the highest of all being Clisham (799m/2620ft) which provides this south-westerly view …

... while to the east, framed by some of the summit rocks, the panorama takes in the great fjord of **35** Loch Seaforth with the region known as Park beyond.

36 Clisham's summit ridge has many outcrops of strangely eroded rocks. The main bedrock of the Outer Hebrides is ancient Lewisian gneiss, formed up to 3,000 million years ago.

The north-westerly view from the ridge takes in the extent of the Harris hills that continue **37**
for about 10 miles before descending to the sea.

38 Compared to the high-level view on p.35, here is a different perspective on Loch Seaforth with moody autumn colours in evidence. This great sea loch extends about 12 miles inland.

Wet weather makes for dramatic waterfalls. Here, on the southern edge of the Harris hills at Bun Abhainn 39
Eadarra on the road to Huisinis, the inevitable consequence of heavy rain is seen to good effect.

40 Continuing towards Huisinis we come to Amhuinnsuidhe Castle. Designed in the Scottish Baronial style by the Victorian architect David Bryce, the Castle was built in 1867 for the 7th Earl of Dunmore.

The port village of Tarbert, Harris. Tarbert is a Norse word meaning a place where boats can be **41** dragged overland between two areas of water. The main ferry route is to Uig, Isle of Skye.

42 The district of South Harris begins at Tarbert. On the west side of South Harris lies Luskentyre where this peaceful, wonderful beach offers rest to the weary and recreation for the young.

The mini-deltas, known as saltings, where rivers and burns meet the sea, are an important habitat 43
for wading birds and wild flowers. The village of Northton is seen in the distance.

44 At the southern tip of South Harris is the village of Rodel, noted for St Clement's Church. Dating to the 1520s, it is built on a site where Christian worship has been practiced for up to 1,500 years.

While the outside is impressive, the carvings housed inside are rated as the finest collection of late 45 medieval sculpture surviving in the Western Isles. This is the tomb of Alexander Macleod.

46 We say farewell to the northern half of the Outer Hebrides as we look back to the village of Leverburgh (named after Lord Leverhulme) from where the ferry crosses the Sound of Harris en route ...

... to Berneray, or strictly speaking the causeway that connects Berneray to North Uist, where the **47** ferry docks. A big Hebridean sky contrasts with the sea, coloured green by the sand beneath.

48 On Berneray, a contrast between restored and unrestored ('would suit DIY enthusiast'!) cottages at the hamlet of Baile – the name is the Gaelic word for township.

The impressive sight of Orcas (also known as Killer Whales) can sometimes be seen in **49** Hebridean waters. Seals are among their favoured prey.

50 As we begin an exploration of North Uist, the first point of interest is the well-preserved Iron Age broch of Dun an Sticir. The picture above shows how two causeways had to be crossed to reach

the broch, seen on the islet on the right, making it a very defensible site. Above is the view across the causeway from the islet on the left of the picture opposite that leads to the broch.

52 Another superb Traigh Mor (Gaelic for big beach), Clachan Sands in the north-facing bay near Trumisgarry, from which the Harris Hills are visible in the distance.

Taking the road that skirts the western side of North Uist brings many delights and also the sight of **53** the somewhat curious folly of Scolpaig Tower, built around 1830 on the site of an earlier dun.

54 Over on the eastern side of North Uist, this view across Loch Blashaval is typical of the landscape on the eastern seaboard of the Uists, where numerous sea lochs encroach inland.

The ferry *Hebrides* makes a fine sight as she approaches Lochmaddy with the service from Uig   **55**
on the Isle of Skye (which is just visible in the background of the picture opposite).

56 Autumn colour warms this grand vista. Taken from Blashaval, it sums up the physical geography of the Uists: water, water everywhere! Here and there outcrops of rocky hills add relief to the scene.

The pair of hills on the right is North and South Lee, neither of them very high but imposing none
the less, given the flatlands that flank them.

58 Here the village of Lochmaddy is seen nestling under the slopes of North Lee. Among Lochmaddy's attractions is Taigh Chearsabhagh, an award-winning Museum and Arts Centre.

South Lee is slightly higher than North Lee, at 281m/921ft. Both can be climbed in a half-day's walk **59** from just outside Lochmaddy. Websites such as www.walkhighlands.co.uk can advise on the route.

60 Although the Outer Hebrides tend to be a windy environment, evening can often bring calmer moments that allow scenes like this. The road from Lochmaddy to Clachan offers many such images.

Further along this road is the huge Barpa Langais chambered cairn, the best preserved in the Outer Hebrides and the only one to retain its original roofed chamber and passage intact.

62 A short distance on (approach via Langais Lodge Hotel) is the largest stone circle in the Uists. Its name, Pobull Fhinn, means Fingal's People, a reference to a hero of early Gaelic literature.

The Uists are rich in ecclesiastical remains. Here the Church of the Holy Trinity at Carinish makes **63** for a peaceful scene at evening. It was an important place of learning in the early medieval period.

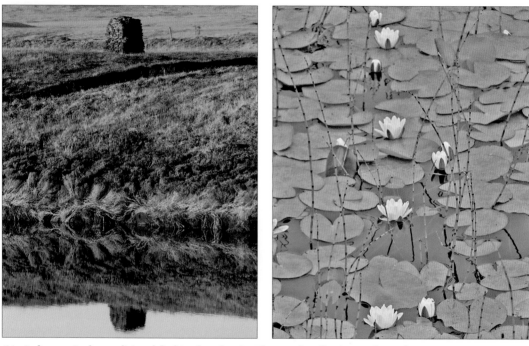

64 Left: peat is the traditional fuel in the islands. This stack will take weeks to dry out.
Right: waterlilies grow in abundance in the Outer Hebrides, seen here in a Benbecula lochan.

Borve Castle, Benbecula, built by the MacRuairis. Its date of construction is not known, but by the middle of the 14th century it was the most important castle in the Outer Hebrides.

66 A little north of Borve, Nunton's beach plays host to a number of oystercatchers. Despite the name, their diet is not limited to oysters.

Left: Further along the beach sanderlings forage for food. **67**
Right: gannets make a spectacular sight as they dive for fish.

68 Left: after crossing the causeway from Benbecula to South Uist the first point of interest is the 9m/30ft tall Our Lady of the Isles statue, erected in 1957. Right: a restored cottage at Howmore.

Loch Druidibeg is one of the larger freshwater lochs on South Uist and is a nature reserve. Beyond, the **69** mountainous triumvirate of Hecla, Beinn Choradail and Beinn Mhor look both appealing and intimidating.

70 At 620m/2034ft Beinn Mhor is the highest point on South Uist and boasts a long and precipitous ridge. For the height of the hill it is quite a tough trek due to the long and boggy walk-in.

To the right of the previous picture, the view south from Beinn Mhor shows how Loch Eynort **71** reaches into the island from the inhospitable east coast.

72 The complex of church and chapel remains at Howmore take on a warm glow in the low evening
sun. It is not known when building began, but the style of an incised stone cross found here suggests

it could have been a place of worship by, or even before, the 9th century. The structure near the
centre of the picture is the remnant of Caibeal Dhiarmaid – St Dermot's Chapel.

74 Just to the north and within sight of the Howmore ruins, Castle Bheagram stands on its island in Loch an Eilein. It is a medieval structure that might have been used as a vantage point or refuge.

Moving a few miles south to Bornais, on a point jutting into the sea is Dun Vulan, an Iron Age broch.
Excavations revealed that what we see now is the remnant of a tower once 4.5m/15ft tall.

76 Left: memorial to Flora MacDonald, born in this area, who went on to aid Bonnie Prince Charlie after Culloden. Right: Beinn a'Charra standing stone is positioned on the slopes that lead to Beinn Mhor.

A pair of roundhouse footings at the Bronze Age settlement of Cladh Hallan near Dalabrog. Occupation of the site goes back to 2200BC, although these structures are more recent, from around 1000BC.

78 The roundhouses on the previous page were part of a larger settlement close to the sea.
The residents could walk down to this beach and watch sunsets like this as often as they wished.

From Dalabrog the main road turns east to reach the village and ferry port of Lochboisdale, seen **79** here from Ben Kenneth. The village was established from about 1838 as a result of land clearances.

80 From Dalabrog one can also continue south to Pollacher. The anglicised version of the village's name comes from the Gaelic, Pol a Charra, which refers to the standing stone here.

Left: the Sound of Eriskay is where the *SS Politician* sank with its cargo of whisky in 1941, the event **81** that inspired the film *Whisky Galore*. Right: the causeway from South Uist to Eriskay.

82 The village of Am Baile on Eriskay. The isle of Eriskay is where Bonnie Prince Charlie first set foot on Scottish soil, in July 1745, having sailed from France.

St Michael's Church in Am Baile (seen at top right opposite) has various links with the sea, including **83** this boat prow built into the altar table. It comes from a lifeboat that belonged to *HMS Hermes*.

84 A 45-minute crossing from Eriskay brings us to Barra where, in the north of the island, are the remains of Cille Bharra, the church of Saint Barr. The surrounding churchyard remains in use.

Barra Airport is the only one in Britain where the runway is the beach! Flight schedules have to take account of the tides. Here, a flight to Glasgow has just lifted off.

86 Its beaches are one of Barra's claims to fame, justifiably so, and this one at Borve on the west of the island is perhaps the best. (With thanks to the ladies in the picture who allowed it to be used.)

Castlebay is the village capital of Barra. Early on a calm summer morning,
this is the tranquil view that greets early risers.

88 Taking time out from our stay on Barra to flit over the causeway to neighbouring Vatersay, we have to indulge in one more beach scene, as the double strands here provide such a tremendous and unusual

view. But of course it's not always like this – there are storms too. Back in 1853 a very severe one caused the emigrant ship *Annie Jane* to strike Vatersay rocks and sink with the loss of 333 lives.

90 Beyond Vatersay a string of small islands continues southwards. The most spectacular of these is Mingulay, with its huge cliffs and sea caves. It can be visited by boat from Barra.

Back on Barra, where superb views of the whole of the island can be enjoyed from Heaval, **91** the 383m/1256ft hill above Castlebay. The Virgin and Child statue looks down over Castlebay.

92 Looking down from Heaval to the east shows a more rugged but still attractive side to the island, where a string of small settlements cluster round the sheltered bays.

Kisimul Castle perches on an islet in Castlebay. The oldest parts still standing may go back to the early 1400s, but the castle has been greatly restored and rebuilt, a task completed in 1970.

94 Castlebay at night. The ferry *Lord of the Isles* has just docked after its voyage of almost five hours from Oban.

The same ferry about to depart the following morning. There are some glum faces on board, **95**
but then, they are about to leave Barra …

Published 2011 by Ness Publishing, 47 Academy Street, Elgin, Moray, IV30 1LR
Phone 01343 549663   www.nesspublishing.co.uk
Reprinted 2012 and 2013

All photographs © Colin Nutt except p.5 (main) © www.virtualheb.co.uk; p.31 © Emma Mitchell;
pp.40 & 90 © Colin Palmer; p.41 © www.undiscoveredscotland.co.uk; p.49 © Andy Foote;
p.67 (right) © Wild Ocean Photography

Text © Colin Nutt
ISBN 978-1-906549-14-5

Front cover: Calanais standing stones; p.1: enjoying Borve beach, Barra; p.4: detail of Virgin and Child statue, Barra;
this page: detail from St Columba's Church gate, Aignish; back cover: Castlebay, Barra.

For a list of websites and phone numbers please turn over >

Websites and phone numbers (where available) for principal places featured in this book in order of appearance:

The Outer Hebrides: www.visithebrides.com/islands
Benbecula: www.isle-of-benbecula.co.uk
St Clement's Church: www.leverburgh.co.uk/stclements
Stornoway: www.stornoway-lewis.co.uk
An Lanntair Arts Centre: www.lanntair.com (T) 01851 703307
Lewis: www.isle-of-lewis.com
St Moluag's Church: www.saintmoluag.com
Arnol Blackhouse: www.historic-scotland.gov.uk (T) 01851 710395
Calanais standing stones: www.callanishvisitorcentre.co.uk (T) 01851 621422
Harris Tweed: www.harristweedhebrides.com (T) 01851 702862
Shawbost Norse Mill: canmore.rcahms.gov.uk
Garenin Blackhouse Village: www.gearrannan.com (T) 01851 643416
Dun Carloway: www.historic-scotland.gov.uk (T) 01851 710395
Harris: www.explore-harris.com
Amhuinnsuidhe Castle: www.amhuinnsuidhe.com (T) 01859 560200
Caledonian Macbrayne: www.calmac.co.uk (T) 0800 066 5000
Harris Tweed Shop: www.isleofharristweedshop.co.uk (T) 01859 502493
North Uist: www.isle-of-north-uist.co.uk
Borve Castle: canmore.rcahms.gov.uk
South Uist: www.southuist.com